HEINEMANN STATE STUDIES

Uniquely
Mississippi

Martin Wilson

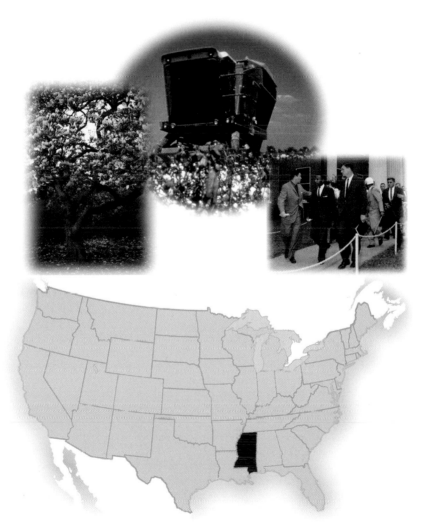

Heinemann Library
Chicago, Illinois

© 2004 Heinemann Library
a division of Reed Elsevier Inc.
Chicago, Illinois

Customer Service   888-454-2279

Visit our website at www.heinemannlibrary.com

Designed by Heinemann Library
Printed in China by WKT Company Limited.

07 06 05 04
10 9 8 7 6 5 4 3 2 1

**Library of Congress
Cataloging-in-Publication Data**

Wilson, Martin, 1973–
    Uniquely Mississippi / Martin Wilson.
        v. cm. -- (Heinemann state studies)
Includes bibliographical references and index.
Contents: Uniquely Mississippi -- Mississippi's
geography and climate -- Famous firsts --
Mississippi's state symbols -- Mississippi's history &
people -- King cotton -- Mississippi's state
government -- Mississippi's culture -- Mississippi's
food -- Mississippi's folklore and legends --
Mississippi's sports teams -- Mississippi's businesses
and products -- Attractions and landmarks.
    ISBN 1-4034-4656-3 (lib. bdg.) --
ISBN 1-4034-4725-X (Pbk.)
    1. Mississippi -- Juvenile literature. [1.
Mississippi.]
I. Title. II. Series.
    F341.3.W55 2004
    976.2 -- dc22

                                    2003025738

Cover Descriptions

Top (left to right) Mississippi state flag,
commercial fishing on Gulf of Mexico,
William Faulkner, cotton field
Main Mississippi paddleboats at Natchez

Acknowledgments

Development and photo research by
BOOK BUILDERS LLC

The author and publishers are grateful to the
following for permission to reproduce copyright
material:

Cover photographs by (top, L-R): Mississippi
Development Authority; Carl Van Vechten/Corbis;
Joe Sohm/Alamy; Debra Ferguson/Alamy; (main):
Andre Jenny/Alamy

Title page (L-R): William Symington/Alamy;
Mississippi Development Authority; Hulton/Getty;
Contents page: Mississippi Development Authority;
p. 4, 13, 27, 28, 30, 40, 44B Mississippi
Development Authority; p. 5, 18 Culver Pictures;
p. 7 David Haggerd/U.S. Fish and Wildlife Service;
p. 8, 36 Courtesy NOAA Photo Library; p. 8, 42,
45 maps by IMA for BOOK BUILDERS LLC; p. 9T,
21, 23, 24, 31, 38 Hulton/Getty; p. 9B Courtesy
Coca-Cola (Coca-Cola is a registered trademark of
the Coca-Cola Co.); p. 10 Courtesy Home of
Heroes; p. 12T Joe Sohm/Alamy; p.12B One Mile
Up; p. 14T, 14M, 14B, 15T, 15B, 25, 27, 32, 39
Alamy; p. 15M Courtesy USFW; p. 16T Fossil
News; p. 16M Animals/Animals; p. 16B Courtesy
U.S. Mint; p. 17 © Sher Hogue, All rights reserved;
p. 18 Culver; p. 20 NY Public Library Picture
Collection; p. 22 AP Wide World; p. 32 Carl Van
Vechten/Corbis; p. 33 Elvis image used by
permission, Elvis Presley Enterprises, Inc.;
p. 34 B. Minton for Heinemann Library;
p. 36 R. Capozzelli/Heinemann Library; p. 37
Courtesy Ole Miss Sports Information; p. 43T
Courtesy Vicksburg National Military Park; p. 43B
Courtesy Mississippi State Society of the Daughters
of the American Revolution or MSSDAR; p. 44T
Courtesy Jefferson Davis Home and Presidential
Library

Special thanks to David Nowak of Mississippi State
University for his comments in the preparation of
this book.

Some words are shown in bold, **like this.**
You can find out what they mean by looking
in the glossary.

Contents

Uniquely Mississippi

When something is *unique,* it is one of a kind. That is certainly true of Mississippi. Mississippi's **Delta** has some of the richest farmland in the country. The Natchez Trace Parkway, which is 444 miles long and more than 8,000 years old, can also be found in the state. Mississippi has also been the home to many great and unique artists and writers, including William Faulkner and Eudora Welty. Thirty-six percent of the people in Mississippi are African American, the largest proportion of African Americans in any state in the country.

ORIGIN OF THE STATE'S NAME

Mississippi got its name from the longest river in North America. The Mississippi River forms the state's western border. In the Ojibwa language, Mississippi means "gathering in of all waters." In Choctaw it means "father of waters." In Algonquin the word means "big river."

MAJOR CITIES

Jackson is the largest city as well as the state capital. It has a population of more than 180,000. Founded as the state capital in 1821, the city is situated on the **bluffs** of the Pearl River. The city was named in honor of Andrew Jackson (1767–1845), who served as president from 1829 to 1837.

The Old Capitol is made entirely of marble, granite, and limestone.

There have been three capitol buildings in Jackson. The first, built in 1822, was only a two-story brick building. The second building, built in 1832 and now called the Old Capitol, is open to the public as a historical museum. It is a superb example of Greek Revival **architecture,** which means it resembles structures first built by the **ancient Greeks.** The current capitol, called the New Capitol, dates from 1903. The Governor's Mansion was completed in 1842, and it is the second-oldest governor's residence in the United States.

Biloxi, which sits on the Gulf Coast, is the state's third-largest city and also one of its oldest. The city was founded by French explorers in 1699 and named for the local Native Americans, the Biloxi. The town served as the capital of the French colonies in the south from 1720 to 1723. When New Orleans became the new capital, Biloxi came under British control in 1763 and under Spanish control in 1779. Biloxi also became part of the **Republic** of West Florida, a short-lived state formed by a group of English and French settlers who did not want to be governed by the Spanish. Once Mississippi became a state in 1812, the city became a resort area. Many southerners were attracted to its coastline and pleasant weather. It is still a tourist attraction today.

Oxford is a small town of about 12,000 people. It is home to the University of Mississippi. The university, also called Ole Miss, opened its doors to 80 students in 1848. Today, when students are in town, the population of Oxford nearly doubles. Many famous writers have called Oxford home, including William Faulkner, who wrote *The Sound and the Fury*, and John Grisham, author of *The Firm.*

The seafood industry played an important part in Biloxi's growth as a city.

Mississippi's Geography and Climate

Mississippi is in the southeastern region of the United States. It ranks 32nd in total area, covering about 48,286 square miles. The Mississippi River forms the state's western boundary, which it shares with Louisiana and Arkansas. To the north the state is bordered by Tennessee, to the east by Alabama, and to the south by Louisiana and the Gulf of Mexico.

THE LAND

Mississippi's land is divided into two geographic regions: the **Alluvial** Plain and the East Gulf Coastal Plain. The Alluvial Plain takes up the western portion of the state. It includes the Delta. The **fertile** soil in this region has been enriched by the mineral deposits from the Mississippi River and others including the Yazoo River and Sunflower River. The soil here is some of the richest in the world, and farms in this region grow cotton and soybeans. The Alluvial Plain also contains many **bayous** and wetlands, low-lying areas that are covered with water. Snakes and alligators make their homes in these wetlands, as do many mosquitoes.

The East Gulf Coastal Plain covers much of eastern Mississippi. The land here consists of low, rolling hills, thick forests, and small **prairies.** The hills are made up of a yellowish-brown soil called loess, which means "soil blown by winds." In the northeastern portion of the state are the Tennessee River Hills. In this region is Woodhall Mountain, which at 806 feet is Mississippi's highest point.

The Mighty Mississippi

The Mississippi River is the third-longest river in the world. It flows for 2,348 miles, from Minnesota to the Gulf of Mexico. The river served as the country's best transportation highway in the 1800s, when many steamboats crowded its waters. Many cities grew along it shores including St. Louis, Memphis, and, in Mississippi, Vicksburg and Natchez. Today, the river is still an important transportation waterway.

The southeastern part of the plain contains the Piney Woods, a hilly area covered with pine trees. The woods here are an important source of lumber for the state.

CLIMATE

The **climate** in Mississippi is mild and **humid,** with short winters and long summers. The average temperature in June is about 80°F. The temperatures in the state rarely rise above 100°F during the summer, mainly because cool, wet winds from the Gulf of Mexico blow across the state. However, it can still seem very hot because of the high humidity. Humidity is the amount of moisture in the air. The temperatures in the winter months average 42°F. Because of the mild weather, farmers in Mississippi have longer growing seasons than states where the weather is colder.

The state's main form of **precipitation** is rain. Snow only falls occasionally in the northern part of Mississippi. The coastal areas are frequently threatened by hurricanes—tropical storms with winds of more than 74 miles per hour that also bring heavy rains, hail, thunder, and lightning. One of the most powerful hurricanes to hit Missis-

Hurricane Camille caused huge waves, many above 25 feet, to flood and destroy more than 45,000 homes.

sippi was Hurricane Camille, which struck the coast on August 17, 1969. Camille carried winds up to 210 miles per hour. These winds destroyed buildings and crops and tore trees out of the ground. The hurricane caused more than 250 deaths and more than $1 billion in damages.

Water from the Gulf of Mexico evaporates and falls as rain. Because of this, more rain falls along the coast.

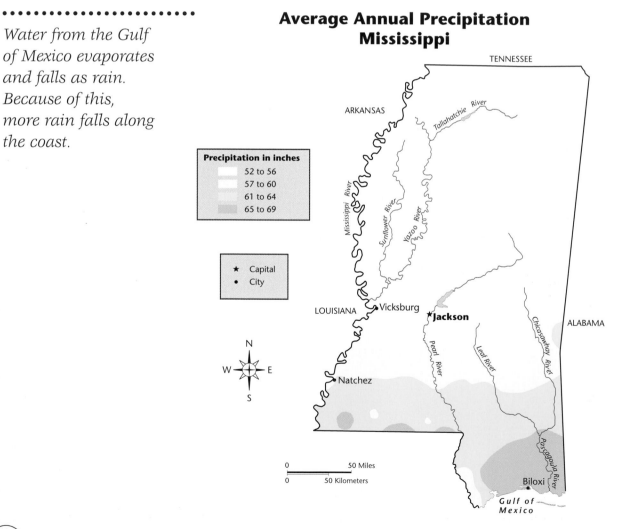

Average Annual Precipitation Mississippi

TENNESSEE

ARKANSAS

Tallahatchie River

Mississippi River

Sunflower River

Yazoo River

Precipitation in inches
- 52 to 56
- 57 to 60
- 61 to 64
- 65 to 69

★ Capital
• City

LOUISIANA

Vicksburg

★**Jackson**

Chickasawhay River

ALABAMA

Pearl River

Leaf River

N
W E
S

Natchez

0   50 Miles
0   50 Kilometers

Pascagoula River

Biloxi

Gulf of Mexico

Famous Firsts

Before he settled in Mississippi, Hiram Revels was a preacher and a school principal in Missouri.

AFRICAN AMERICAN FIRSTS

In 1870 Hiram Revels of Natchez became the first African American to serve in the U.S. Senate. He completed Jefferson Davis's term. Davis was the former president of the **Confederacy.**

Blanche Kelso Bruce of Bolivar County was the first African American to serve an entire term in the U.S. Senate. He served from 1875 to 1880. During his term, he became the first African American to **preside** over a Senate session. After he left the Senate, he held the office of **register** of the U.S. Treasury from 1881 to 1885.

Alcorn State University in Rodney is the oldest college for African Americans on land granted from the government. The state legislature gave the college $50,000 and 225 acres of land to establish the college in 1871. Hiram Revels became the university's first president after he completed his senate term in 1871. Today, the college sits on about 1,700 acres of land.

SOFT DRINK FIRSTS

In 1894 Joe Biedenharn of Vicksburg was the first person to bottle the soft drink Coca-Cola.

Thanks to Biedenharn, people living in rural areas could obtain Coca-Colas for the first time.

The Youngest Medal of Honor Winner

Jack Lucas of Hattiesburg is the youngest person ever to win the Congressional Medal of Honor. Lucas, only seventeen years old at the time, lied about his age to enlist in the marines. He stowed away on a troopship to get to the fighting war in the Pacific in World War II (1939–1945). He and three other marines were patrolling the island of Iwo Jima, which was occupied by the Japanese, when they were suddenly attacked with grenades. To protect the other marines from injury or death from the explosions, Lucas threw himself on top of the grenades. His body took the force of the whole blast. Somehow he survived. He underwent surgery 22 times, and doctors removed more than 200 pieces of **shrapnel** from his body. Lucas received his medal for astonishing bravery from President Harry Truman on October 5, 1945.

Before then, people could only drink sodas at a soda fountain store. Biedenharn thought it would be great if people could drink Coca-Cola wherever and whenever they wanted. In the summer of 1894 he began to bottle Coca-Cola.

MEDICAL FIRSTS

In 1963 the University of Mississippi Medical Center performed the world's first human lung transplant. Physicians took the lung from one person and placed it into the body of another person. James D. Hardy led the team that performed the operation. In 1964 Hardy performed the world's first heart transplant surgery. He and his team transplanted the heart of a chimpanzee into a dying man. The man's new heart beat for about 90 minutes before it stopped. These two operations paved the way for future transplants, which continue to this day with much success.

MILITARY FIRSTS

The Congressional Medal of Honor is the highest award that can be given to a person serving in the Armed Services of the United States. It is awarded for **valor** in action against an enemy force. During **World War II,** seven Mississippians won the medal, more than service people from any other state.

CULTURAL FIRSTS

The teddy bear has its origins in Mississippi. President Theodore "Teddy" Roosevelt visited the state in 1902 and went on a hunting trip in Sharkey County. During the hunt, he refused to shoot a bear cub. A cartoon that ran in a national newspaper showed Roosevelt and the helpless bear. A couple in Brooklyn, New York, created a stuffed bear in honor of the president, and they called it "Teddy's Bear." Eventually their stuffed animal caught on and the teddy bear was born.

Mississippi's State Symbols

MISSISSIPPI STATE FLAG

The state legislature appointed a committee to design the state flag in 1894. In the upper left corner is a reproduction of the Confederate flag, which is a reminder of the state's membership in the **Confederacy.** The thirteen stars represent the original thirteen colonies of the United States.

The state flag features red, white, and blue stripes, which are the national colors.

MISSISSIPPI STATE SEAL

The state seal was adopted in 1817. It features an eagle with its wings spread and its head pointing upward. The thirteen stars and stripes on the shield represent the original thirteen colonies. The arrows that

Mississippi has used the basic design of the current seal since 1798, when it was still a territory.

the eagle holds symbolize the ability to wage war. The eagle also holds an olive branch, which symbolizes the desire for peace.

STATE SONG: "GO MISSISSIPPI"

The state adopted "Go Mississippi" by Houston Davis as the state song in 1962.

STATE MOTTO: *VIRTUTE ET ARMIS*

The state motto is *Virtute et armis,* which means "By valor and arms." The motto was suggested by James Rhea Preston, the state superintendent of education, in 1894.

STATE NICKNAME: MAGNOLIA STATE

The nickname, "The Magnolia State," pays tribute to the beauty of Mississippi's magnolia trees. The tree can be found throughout the state.

STATE FLOWER: MAGNOLIA

Elementary school students chose the magnolia as the state flower in 1900. The state legislature did not approve the measure until 1952. The flowers can be found across the state.

"Go, Mississippi"

Words and Music by Houston Davis

States may sing their songs of praise
With waving flags and hip-hoo-rays,
Let cymbals crash and let bells ring
'Cause here's one song I'm proud to sing.

Choruses

Go, Mississippi, keep rolling along,
Go, Mississippi, you cannot go wrong,
Go, Mississippi, we're singing your song,
M-I-S-S-I-S-S-I-P-P-I
Go, Mississippi, you're on the right track,
Go, Mississippi, and this is a fact,
Go, Mississippi, you'll never look back,
M-I-S-S-I-S-S-I-P-P-I
Go, Mississippi, straight down the line,
Go, Mississippi, ev'rything's fine,
Go, Mississippi, it's your state and mine,
M-I-S-S-I-S-S-I-P-P-I

Inside every magnolia blossom is a cone-shaped fruit.

Magnolia trees can grow up to 90 feet tall. The tree's leaves are large, long, leathery, glossy, and of a dark-green color.

STATE TREE: MAGNOLIA TREE

School children selected the magnolia tree as the state tree in 1935, but the legislature did not make it official until 1938. Magnolias thrive in rich, moist soil, which is why they are so common in Mississippi.

STATE BIRD: MOCKINGBIRD

The mockingbird was named the state bird in 1944. It was selected by the members of the Federated Women's Clubs. Mockingbirds are found all over the state. They are known for their ability to copy, or mock, the songs of other birds. They can copy other sounds, too, including dogs!

Mockingbirds like to live in high perches, so the male mockingbird can sing and defend his territory.

STATE LAND ANIMAL: WHITE-TAILED DEER

The white-tailed deer was named the state land mammal in 1974 because they are common in Mississippi. Their white tails can be one foot in length. They prefer to live in forests and swamps. In the winter, they live with other deer, but they like to live alone in the warmer months.

White-tailed deer can live from fifteen to twenty years.

Largemouth bass can weigh up to twenty pounds or more.

STATE FISH: LARGEMOUTH BASS

The largemouth bass, also called the black bass, is a common fish in Mississippi's lakes, creeks, and swamps. The largemouth bass was named Mississippi's state fish in 1974.

STATE WATERFOWL: WOOD DUCK

In 1974 Mississippi chose the wood duck as its state waterfowl. These ducks live near the rivers, lakes, and ponds of Mississippi. The wood duck is a popular game bird with hunters.

STATE WATER MAMMAL: BOTTLE-NOSE DOLPHIN

The bottle-nose dolphin was named Mississippi's state water mammal in 1974. These dolphins are small, toothed whales. They have a long, beaklike snout, which is how they got their name. Dolphins breathe through a blowhole. They live in the oceans in **temperate** climates, including off the coast of Mississippi. They can grow to be twelve feet long.

Wood ducks nest in trees such as bald cypresses and sycamores.

Dolphins stay in small groups, or "pods," of up to 12 whales and can live for about 25 years.

15

The whales were 45 to 70 feet in length with wedge-shaped heads that were about 5 feet long. They did not really look like the whales of today.

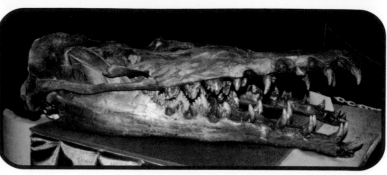

STATE FOSSIL: PREHISTORIC WHALE

The **fossilized** remains of prehistoric whales were first discovered in Mississippi, Alabama, and Louisiana in the 1840s. The whale, also referred to as *basilosaurus,* lived 35 to 40 million years ago, when what is now Mississippi was covered by an ocean. The prehistoric whale fossil was named the state fossil in 1981.

STATE STONE: PETRIFIED WOOD

Mississippi named petrified wood as the state stone in 1976. Mississippi is home to the only petrified forest east of the Rocky Mountains.

The petrified forest was formed more than 36 million years ago. The logs were buried in the sandy soil of Flora, Mississippi.

MISSISSIPPI STATE QUARTER

The Mississippi state quarter was released by the U.S. Mint in 2002. It was the twentieth coin to be issued, because Mississippi was the twentieth state to enter the Union. The quarter shows a magnolia, which is the state flower and tree. The quarter also features the state's nickname: The Magnolia State.

The date 1817 represents the year that Mississippi was admitted to the Union.

Mississippi's History and People

Mississippi's history includes native people, European explorers and later settlers, and enslaved Africans brought to North America to work the land.

EARLY PEOPLES

Mississippi's earliest inhabitants were Mound Builders who lived about 12,000 years ago throughout what is now Mississippi. Though these people left no written records, **archeologists** have found many of their **artifacts,** including tools and pottery. These people built large mounds, many of which still stand today. Archeologists think the mounds were used for religious ceremonies. The largest mound is Emerald Mound, which can be found near Natchez. They are believed to have built the Natchez Trace, the 500-mile route that runs from what is now Mississippi to Tennessee. Hunters were the first to use it. Later it became an important trade route.

The Natchez Trace is the oldest road in North America.

The Choctaw, Chickasaw, and Natchez tribes were living in Mississippi when European explorers arrived during the 1500s. The Natchez were probably **descendants** of the Mound Builders. They hunted, fished, and raised corn, squash, and beans in southwestern Mississippi.

EUROPEAN EXPLORERS AND SETTLERS

European explorers and settlers have influenced Mississippi's history heavily. The first European to reach Mississippi was Hernando de Soto, then governor of the Spanish colony of Cuba. De Soto and his men became the first Europeans to see the Mississippi River when searching for gold in 1539. He returned to the river in 1542, but came down with a fever and died. He is buried in the Mississippi near Natchez.

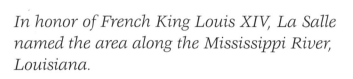

In honor of French King Louis XIV, La Salle named the area along the Mississippi River, Louisiana.

In 1682, the French arrived in Mississippi. The explorer La Salle traveled down the river from Canada and claimed the land for France. In the 1700s the British challenged French claims. In 1754 they went to war. When the **French and Indian War** (1754–1763) ended, the British controlled almost all of the land east of the Mississippi River. They divided much of what is now Mississippi between two colonies. The southern part was called West Florida. The rest belonged to Georgia.

ROAD TO STATEHOOD

In the 1760s and 1770s, the American colonists began to grow restless under British control. The colonists wanted independence. During the **Revolutionary War**

(1775–1783), the British gave West Florida to Spain. When Americans won their independence in 1783, the land north of the 32nd parallel became part of the new United States, while the land south of the 31st parallel belonged to Spain. The territory of Mississippi was formed in 1798, with Natchez as the capital. Winthrop Sargent was appointed as the first governor.

In 1817 Congress divided the Mississippi Territory into the state of Mississippi and Alabama Territory. Jackson became the state capital in 1822. During this time, Native Americans were forced to give up their lands and move farther west.

Civil War

Mississippi entered the Union at a time when cotton was becoming the nation's leading crop. The new state's rich soil soon attracted farmers eager to grow cotton. Some built large **plantations** that relied on enslaved labor. By 1860 enslaved African Americans outnumbered white Americans in Mississippi.

Throughout the early 1800s, the issue of slavery divided the nation. A growing number of states in the North had ended slavery and they did not want it spread to newly formed states in the West. White southerners saw slavery as central to their way of life, even though most of them did not own slaves. A turning point came in 1860 when Abraham Lincoln, who opposed slavery, was elected president. Within weeks of his victory, many states in the South decided to **secede** from the Union. The first to leave the Union was South Carolina in late 1860. Mississippi became the second on January 9, 1861. Other southern states joined them, forming the **Confederacy,** or the Confederate States of America. Jefferson Davis, a U.S. senator from Mississippi, became the president of the Confederacy. The **Civil War** began in April 1861.

Many of the Confederate soldiers and people of Vicksburg starved during the Battle of Vicksburg.

The fighting came to Mississippi after the Battle of Shiloh in 1862. Shiloh is in Tennessee, just north of Mississippi. The Confederates, who were defeated there, fled to Corinth, Mississippi, a major railroad town. Union troops followed and defeated the Confederates. They took over the town and gained control of the major railways in the state.

The Union army next targeted Vicksburg. Because the city is on the Mississippi River, it was a key center for trade. The South needed the river to transport supplies. In 1862 and 1863, U.S. General Ulysses S. Grant and his troops surrounded the city, blocking anyone from getting in or out. Supplies such as weapons and food became scarce. The **siege** of the city lasted 47 days and claimed the lives of 10,000 soldiers from both sides. The surrender of Confederate General John C. Pemberton on July 4, 1863, was a turning point in the Civil War, because it weakened the South severely. The war finally came to an end in 1865.

RECONSTRUCTION

The Civil War ended in 1865 with a Union victory. Soon after, slavery ended, and Mississippi, like other Confederate states, was placed under military rule. In December 1869, Mississippians passed a new constitution that granted blacks the right to vote. On February 23, 1870, the state was allowed to return to the Union. For a time, African Americans not only voted in Mississippi but also held government jobs. Many white Mississippians refused to share power with black Mississippians. In 1890 they took over the government and created a new constitution that denied voting rights to most African Americans. Soon after, Mississippi passed laws that called for **segregation** in schools and other public places. The late 1800s and early 1900s saw the rise of a group called the Ku Klux Klan. Members terrorized African Americans—particularly those who tried to exercise their rights as citizens.

CIVIL RIGHTS

Although African Americans challenged segregation, they made little progress until after **World War II** (1939–1945). In 1954, the U.S. Supreme Court declared that segregation was not "separate but equal" and was thus unconstitutional. Even though the ruling in this case, *Brown* vs. *Board of Education,* was about a lawsuit in Kansas, this decision affected other states where segregation persisted, including Mississippi.

The civil rights movement in Mississippi gained strength in the late 1950s through the 1960s. Blacks and white came from all over to protest segregation and violence against African Americans. In 1962 James Howard Meredith became the first African American student admitted to the

Due to the riots and violence, federal troops remained on Ole Miss's campus until James Meredith graduated in 1963.

Emmett Till

Emmett Till, a fourteen-year-old African American boy from Chicago, visited his relatives in Money, Mississippi, in the summer of 1955. Till was unprepared for the kind of treatment African Americans experienced in Mississippi and other southern states. While in a local store buying candy, he talked to and maybe even whistled at a white woman named Carol Bryant. Her husband, Roy Bryant, owned the store. To Emmett, this was not unusual, but in Mississippi it was unheard of for a black boy to talk to a white woman without being spoken to first. Two days later, Roy Bryant and J.W. Milam, his brother-in-law, found Emmett at his uncle's house and kidnapped him. On August 27, Emmett was beaten to death. His body was thrown into the Tallahatchie River. After his body was found, it was shipped back to Chicago for burial. The murder shocked the nation and outraged blacks. The two men were tried for the murder, and many courageous African Americans testified. But in the end Bryant and Milam were **acquitted** by the all-white jury. This enraged people throughout the country. The event became a turning point in the national and local civil rights movement.

University of Mississippi. But the governor at the time, Ross Barnett, refused to let him enter. Students at Ole Miss rioted and federal troops had to come in to bring about peace and order. Meredith was finally admitted on October 1, 1962. This was an important moment in the Civil Rights Movement in Mississippi. In 1964 Mississippi's elementary and high schools started the process of desegregation, though sometimes the process took many years.

In 1965 Congress passed the Voting Rights Act at the request of President Lyndon B. Johnson. The new law protected the right of African Americans to take part in local, state, and national elections. This act changed the political situation in Mississippi, as the vote from African Americans often became crucial in many elections. The road to equality continues in the state, but today about twenty percent of state legislators are African American.

FAMOUS PEOPLE

Ida B. Wells-Barnett (1862–1931), journalist. Wells-Barnett, the daughter of slaves, was born in Holly Springs. She grew up to be a teacher in Memphis and started and wrote for a paper for blacks called *Living War.* She later wrote for *Memphis Free Speech* and became a strong, outspoken voice for the rights of African Americans. She was one of the original founders of the **National Association for the Advancement of Colored People (NAACP).**

Ida B. Wells-Barnett led the effort to abolish lynching in the United States.

Walter Anderson (1903–1965), artist, painter. Anderson was born in New Orleans but grew up and spent much of his life in Ocean Springs. He studied at many fine art schools in both the United States and Europe before returning to Mississippi. He spent a lot of time painting on Horn Island. Living alone in a cottage, he drew animals, birds, insects, and plants that were native to the region. When he died, his relatives found his paintings spread throughout his cottage.

Medgar Evers (1925–1963), social activist. Born in Decatur, Evers served as the first field secretary for the NAACP in Mississippi. Among many of his achievements for the civil rights cause, he helped get James Meredith admitted to Ole Miss. His actions angered many opponents to civil rights. In 1963 he was shot and killed outside of his home in Jackson.

B.B. King (1925–   ), musician. King was born in Itta Bena and became a famous **blues** singer and electric guitarist. He earned the nickname "King of Blues." **Gospel music** influenced his singing style. Some of his famous songs include "Lucille" and "The Thrill is Gone." He was inducted into the Blues Foundation Hall of Fame in 1984 and into the Rock and Roll Hall of Fame in 1986.

Jim Henson (1936–1990), puppeteer. Born in Greenville, Henson started working with puppets from an early age. His first puppet shows appeared on television in Maryland in 1955. In 1969 his "muppets" such as Bert and Ernie and Big Bird became famous on the show *Sesame Street.* Later he created *The Muppet Show,* which featured Kermit the Frog and Miss Piggy.

Oprah Winfrey's women's magazine, O., the Oprah Magazine, *debuted in 2000.*

Oprah Winfrey (1954–   ), talk-show host, actor. Born in Kosciusko, Winfrey went to college in Tennessee and later worked as a television reporter in Nashville. In 1983 she started a local talk show in Chicago. She first gained national notice when she appeared in the 1985 movie *The Color Purple,* for which she was nominated for an **Oscar.** That same year her talk show, called *The Oprah Winfrey Show,* went national and became one of the top-rated programs in the country.

John Grisham (1955–   ), novelist. Grisham, who grew up in Southaven, is one of the country's best-selling authors. His books, including *The Firm* and *The Client,* have sold millions of copies. He started writing while he was working as a lawyer. Many of his books draw on his experiences as a lawyer.

King Cotton

In the late 1700s and early 1800s, farmers from other Southern states started moving to Mississippi because of its rich, unspoiled farmland. Cotton grew well in Mississippi. However, separating the seeds from the fibers was difficult and unprofitable because it was done by hand. As such, little cotton was grown in Mississippi.

THE RISE OF COTTON

The cotton gin, invented by Eli Whitney in 1793, made cotton production easier and quicker because the machine separated the seeds from the fibers. However, landowners still depended on slaves to do the harvesting, and it was hard work.

By the 1830s cotton was the country's chief export. Before the boom in cotton production, slaves accounted for a small percentage of the state's population. By 1850 three out of every four people in the larger cotton-growing areas such as Natchez were slaves. By 1860 more than 400,000 slaves lived in the state.

In 1830, Mississippi produced 387,000 bales of cotton, more than any other state.

Cotton was so important to Mississippi and its economy that the state acquired the nickname "King Cotton." Natchez became the leading cotton center. Cotton bales were shipped down the Mississippi to the Gulf, and then transported to Europe. Many landowners became very wealthy from selling their cotton to clothing manufacturers in the North and abroad. They were able to maintain their prosperity because the hard manual labor was done by slaves, not by paid laborers.

Landowners built mansions on their **plantations.** These **antebellum** mansions were often huge and luxurious. On the other hand, small farms were actually more common, and many white farmers harvested their own cotton without the help of slaves.

COTTON AFTER THE CIVIL WAR

Few landowners worried about relying on a single crop for their livelihood. Many thought that cotton would make them rich forever. After the **Civil War** (1861–1865), slavery was outlawed, and some of the huge plantations were broken up into small farms. Former slaves became tenant farmers, or sharecroppers, farming on land owned by their former masters. For the right to farm the land, these tenant farmers and sharecroppers often gave half the crop to the landowner as rent. They also had to borrow money to buy farming supplies, which increased their debts. Sharecropping was a hard life. There was a lot of work and not much financial reward. Thousands of African Americans left the cotton farms of the South and migrated to the north for a better life, especially during the **Great Depression** in the early 1930s. African Americans also left because of the invention of the mechanical cotton picker, which decreased the need for human labor.

Farmers now use tractors and other machines to harvest cotton, eliminating some of the difficult manual labor.

In 1907 an insect called the boll weevil first invaded farms in Mississippi. Over a period of seven years, boll weevils infested cotton farms throughout the state, destroying many crops and causing farms to close down. It is estimated that boll weevils caused $13 billion of damage to the cotton industry before they were completely wiped out in the late 1970s.

The presence of the boll weevil forced many farmers to rely on other crops, such as corn, rice, wheat, and soybeans. However, Mississippi still relies heavily on cotton. In 2003 more than one million acres of cotton were harvested. This harvest produced 2.18 million bales of cotton, which was the third-largest cotton crop in the United States.

Mississippi's State Government

Like the U.S. government, Mississippi's government is divided into three branches: legislative, executive, and judicial. Also like the U.S. government, Mississippi has a constitution, which is a document that includes the basic laws and principles of the state government. The constitution also grants certain rights, including the right to vote. The state government is centered in Jackson, the state capital.

The current state capitol in Jackson was built in 1903. There were two earlier capitol buildings, and one of them, the Old Capitol in Jackson, is now a museum. Both the legislative and executive branches are housed in the current capitol.

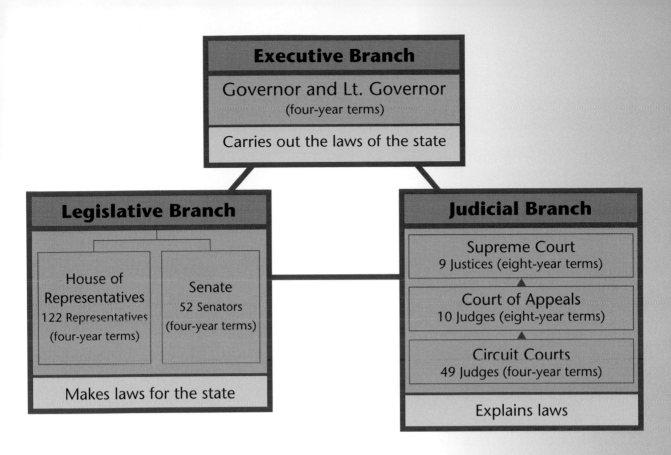

Executive Branch

Governor and Lt. Governor
(four-year terms)

Carries out the laws of the state

Legislative Branch

House of Representatives
122 Representatives
(four-year terms)

Senate
52 Senators
(four-year terms)

Makes laws for the state

Judicial Branch

Supreme Court
9 Justices (eight-year terms)

Court of Appeals
10 Judges (eight-year terms)

Circuit Courts
49 Judges (four-year terms)

Explains laws

LEGISLATIVE BRANCH

The legislative branch of Mississippi makes the laws. In Mississippi, the legislature is divided into two houses—the senate and the house of representatives. Before a **bill** can become a law, both houses must support it. The bill is then sent to the governor for approval. If the governor decides to **veto** the bill, it can still become law if a two-thirds majority in both houses votes to override the veto. The legislature also approves state budgets prepared by the governor.

The state's 52 senators and 122 representatives serve four-year terms. The state legislature meets for 90 days each year. In years when a governor is elected, the sessions last 125 days.

EXECUTIVE BRANCH

The executive branch enforces state laws in Mississippi. The governor heads the executive branch. The governor is elected for a four-year term. Until 1988, governors could not serve consecutive terms, but now the governor can serve two terms in a row. He or she is also in charge of developing policies for the economy, law, and education.

Other elected officials in the executive branch are the treasurer, secretary of state, attorney general, and lieutenant governor. These officials also serve four-year terms and help run the state.

Judicial Branch

The judicial branch applies the state's laws to particular cases. There are three levels of courts in Mississippi. The lowest courts are chancery or circuit courts. The judges in these courts hear civil and criminal cases. Civil cases involve disputes among private citizens over such matters as property rights, contracts, and child custody. Criminal cases are instances where someone has broken a law. Robbery is a criminal case.

The next level of courts is the court of appeals. It handles cases in which a decision of the lower court has been challenged or appealed. These courts decide whether to uphold or overturn the earlier decision. The court of appeals has ten judges who are elected to eight-year terms.

The judicial branch of the government is housed in the Gartin Justice Building.

The state's highest court is the supreme court. The Mississippi Supreme Court consists of nine justices, who are elected to eight-year terms. The justice who has served the longest time is the chief justice. The supreme court hears cases that have been appealed at lower levels.

Mississippi's Culture

Mississippi is famous for its writers and musicians. They have contributed to the cultural life of Mississippi, the United States, and the world.

MISSISSIPPI WRITERS

One of the state's most beloved writers was Jackson-born Eudora Welty (1909–2001). Welty's novels and short stories focused on Mississippi and its people. She won many awards throughout her career, including the **Pulitzer Prize,** the Presidential Medal of Freedom, and the National Book Foundation's Medal for Distinguished Contribution to American Letters. Some of her most famous novels include *The Optimist's Daughter* and *Losing Battles.* She is probably best known for her short stories, including "Why I Live at the P.O." All of her writings are marked by her sharp wit, ear for dialogue, and colorful portraits of life in both urban and rural Mississippi.

The state's largest public library in Jackson is named after Eudora Welty.

Richard Wright (1908–1960), the son of a sharecropper, was born in Natchez. His novels and short stories drew on his experiences as an African American in the South. His most famous works are *Native Son,* published in 1940, and *Black Boy,* written in 1945. Wright eventually moved to Paris, France, where he died in 1960. *Native Son* is ranked 20th on the Modern Library's list of the "100 Best Novels of the 20th Century."

Three of William Faulkner's novels—As I Lay Dying, The Sound and the Fury, Light in August—*made the Modern Library's list of the "100 Best Novels of the 20th Century."*

The playwright Tennessee Williams (1911–1983) was also born in Mississippi. He grew up in Columbus. His plays, many of which are set in the South, are performed all over the world. Two of his most famous plays, *A Streetcar Named Desire* and *The Glass Menagerie,* were made into award-winning films. Like Welty, he won the Presidential Medal of Freedom.

Perhaps the best-known and most unique writer from Mississippi was William Faulkner (1897–1962). Born in New Albany, Faulkner eventually settled in Oxford. He set many of his novels and short stories in a fictional Mississippi county, Yoknapatawpha County. His most famous novels are *As I Lay Dying, The Sound and the Fury,* and *Light in August.* The books are powerful explorations of love, family, race, and the way past events in Mississippi's history shaped people's lives. Faulkner won the Pulitzer Prize twice, in 1955 and 1963. He also won the **Nobel Prize for Literature** in 1949, the highest international honor for writers.

Rowan Oak

William Faulkner wrote many of his novels in his home in Oxford, which he named Rowan Oak. Its name comes from a Scottish legend that claimed that rowan wood kept away evil spirits. The house was originally built in the 1840s and Faulkner bought it in 1930.

Faulkner did his writing in his home office. He even planned out one of his novels, *A Fable,* in pencil on the office walls. The writing can still be seen. Today, the house is a museum, open to the public.

MISSISSIPPI MUSICIANS

Mississippi has been the home to many world-famous musicians. The state has produced many **blues** singers and musicians, in particular.

Blues music has its roots in African culture, and developed on southern **plantations** among slaves. Blues songs are slow in tempo, and the songs are about work and love and human suffering. Some of the best-known blues musicians to come from Mississippi were Muddy Waters, Robert Johnson, and B.B. King (see page 24). Muddy Waters (1915–1983), born in Rolling Fork, was famous for his singling style, which sounded a lot like shouting and moaning. He won six Grammy Awards.

Born in Hazlehurst, Robert Johnson (1911–1938) became known as the King of the **Delta** Blues. He died young and only recorded 29 songs. But these songs, including "Love in Vain" and "Crossroads," inspired many future musicians, including rock and country artists. He was inducted into the Rock and Roll Hall of Fame in 1986. Each September, Greenville is host to the Delta Blues Festival.

Another important Mississippi-born musician was Elvis Presley (1935–1977). Presley was born in Tupelo and became one of the most famous and loved rock-and-roll performers of all time. His songs combined elements of country, rhythm and blues, and rock and roll. He gained fame in 1956 when his album *Heartbreak Hotel* topped the national charts for eight weeks. Some of his famous hit songs include "Don't Be Cruel" and "Love Me Tender." Presley also starred in many popular movies. He became known as the King of Rock and Roll.

Six of Elvis Presley's songs are included on the Rock and Roll Hall of Fame's "500 Songs That Shaped Rock and Roll" list.

Mississippi's Food

The rich farmland of the Delta produces many vegetables and animals from which Mississippians have always made a wide variety of dishes. Frying foods is common in Mississippi, giving dishes a rich and juicy taste. Mississippians fry things such as okra, green tomatoes, and of course chicken. But Mississippians have always loved sweets, including Mississippi Mud Cake.

Mississippi Mud Cake

Be sure to have an adult help you!

2 sticks margarine	1 teaspoon vanilla
½ cup milk	1½ cups pecans, chopped
½ cup cocoa	dash of salt
4 eggs	1 small package of
1½ cups self-rising flour	miniature marshmallows
2 cups sugar	

Melt the margarine in a bowl. Add cocoa with beaten eggs, flour, and milk. Add salt and sugar. Beat well, then add the nuts and beat more. Pour this batter into a greased pan (13 X 9 X 2 inches). Bake for 35 minutes at 350°F. Pour marshmallows over the cake while it is still hot. Put cake in oven until marshmallows melt. Either make your own icing or buy icing in a store. Spread icing over marshmallows once the cake has cooled.

Mississippi's Folklore and Legends

Legends and folklore are stories that are often based on bits of truth. Often these stories help people understand things that cannot be easily explained. They also teach lessons to younger generations.

THE SINGING RIVER

The Pascagoula lived near the river that bears their name, the Pascagoula River. Legend has it that Anola, a princess of the Biloxi tribe, was in love with Altama, a young chief of the Pascagoula tribe. She ran away from her tribe to be with him. Because of this, the Biloxi grew angry and wanted to enslave the Pascagoula. The Pascagoula could not bear this, so legend has it that they disappeared into the waters of the river, never to be seen again. As they went underwater, they sang and chanted some of their tribal songs.

Some people say that you can still hear the Pascagoula singing as the river waters flow by. Thus, the river is called "The Singing River."

MISSISSIPPI MOSQUITOES

A visitor to Mississippi decided to take a walk along the banks of the Mississippi River. A native Mississippian warned him about the mosquitoes.

"The mosquitoes are acting real bad lately. Real bad! They even drove the alligators upriver," the man said. "They're biting like crazy."

"Oh, please. Mosquitoes? No mosquito is going to keep me from my walk," the visitor said.

As the visitor walked along the river, he suddenly heard a high-pitched, whiny sound—much like the sound of a tornado. The sound was coming from two mosquitoes, who were heading straight toward him. Before he knew it, the mosquitoes had lifted him into the air and were carrying him across the river.

"Shall we bite bit him here or in the swamp?" one mosquito asked the other.

"Oh, let's bite him here. I'm hungry," said the other.

Terrified, the man kicked, screamed, and fought until the mosquitoes lost their grip and dropped him into the river. Eventually he washed up on shore, downriver. He left Mississippi immediately, and never took another walk again. If only he had listened to the advice of his Mississippi friend!

Mississippi's Sports Teams

Mississippians love sports, and many of their teams have achieved much national success.

COLLEGE TEAMS

Mississippi is home to many collegiate sports teams. The teams of the University of Mississippi, or Ole Miss, in Oxford and Mississippi State in Starkville belong to the Southeastern Conference (SEC), which has a tradition of strong athletic teams in many sports. Southern Mississippi University in Hattiesburg also fields strong athletic teams. The Ole Miss football team has won the Sugar Bowl five times, and Mississippi State has won numerous bowls as well, including the Orange Bowl. In 1999 all three teams won their bowl games for the first time in the state's history—the Peach Bowl for Mississippi State, the Liberty Bowl for Southern Mississippi, and the Independence Bowl for Ole Miss. In 2004 Ole Miss won the Cotton Bowl. Ole Miss has also been the SEC champion six times.

The Mississippi State men's baseball team has also been very successful. The Mississippi State Bulldogs have been the SEC champion ten times, and they have won the College World Series seven times, most recently in 1998.

Ole Miss' Eli Manning won the 2003 Maxwell Award for the country's most outstanding college football player.

MISSISSIPPI HOCKEY

Hockey may not be the first thing that comes to mind when Mississippi sports are discussed, but the Mississippi Sea Wolves are a popular minor league hockey team in Biloxi. The team plays in front of large crowds at the Mississippi Coast Coliseum and is often in the running for the title of the East Coast Hockey League (ECHL). Bob Woods, the current coach, has one of the highest winning percentages of any coach in the history of the league. He was also a popular player for the team. His No. 8 jersey hangs high in the Coliseum in tribute to his play and contributions to the community.

Mississippi's NFL Greats

Mississippi is the home to many top players in the National Football League (NFL). Brett Favre was born in 1969 in Pass Christian, but he grew up in Kiln and went to Southern Mississippi. He led the Green Bay Packers to a Super Bowl victory in 1996, defeating the New England Patriots 35–21. Favre won the NFL Most Valuable Player award in 1997. Walter Payton (1954–1999) of Columbia went to Jackson State. He is the NFL's second All-Time Leading Rusher. He also scored a career total of 125 touchdowns, which put him in fifth place of all time. He is one of the greatest running backs of all time and was elected to the Pro Football Hall of Fame. Jerry Rice of Crawford went to Mississippi Valley State and has won three Super Bowl titles while playing with the San Francisco 49ers. He has also scored the most touchdowns of any player in NFL history—205. He is considered the greatest wide receiver to ever play the game.

Mississippi's Businesses and Products

Mississippi's economy was once based almost solely on cotton. But over the years, other businesses and industries have taken an important and vital role in the economy.

FARM PRODUCTS

Cotton is still the principal crop in Mississippi. In 2002, cotton was planted on more than 1.2 million acres of land. These cotton crops were worth about $340 million to the state economy. Most of the state's cotton is grown in the northeastern part of the state. Mississippi ranks third in the nation in all cotton production. Soybeans are the next most important crop to the state, followed by rice, corn, cottonseed, and sweet potatoes.

Poultry, which includes chicken and turkey, is a billion-dollar industry in the state. Chickens, also called broilers (chickens that are five to twelve weeks old), are raised on Mississippi farms for the meat and eggs they produce. The poultry industry has grown by 80 percent since 1989

Poultry is Mississippi's top farm product.

Biloxi is Mississippi's main shrimp-packing port.

and employs more than 20,000 workers. In 2003 the state's chicken and eggs were worth more than $1.5 billion. Mississippi ranks fourth in the nation in poultry products. One of the top poultry companies in the state is Tyson Foods. Most of the poultry farms can be found in the area between Hattiesburg, Jackson, and Meridian.

FISHING

Mississippi is now the nation's leading producer of catfish. The catfish are grown in human-made ponds. In 1999 Mississippi accounted for more than 60 percent of the catfish market in the United States. More than 106,000 acres of water are used for catfish production. Sales of catfish earned the state almost $300 million in 1999.

The Gulf Coast is also the site of some of the nation's busiest **ports.** Pascagoula handled about 27.5 million tons of cargo in 1998, making it the 23rd-busiest port in the country. The Gulf also attracts many commercial fishers. The main fishing catches include shrimp, sea trout, flounder, tuna, oysters, and red snapper. Most of the commercial fish are handled at the port at Pascagoula, one of the nation's largest commercial fishing ports.

INDUSTRY AND MANUFACTURING

Many national corporations have factories, plants, or headquarters in Mississippi. Among these corporations are WorldCom, one of the nation's leading long-distance **telecommunication** companies. WorldCom is based in Jackson. Other corporations include General Electric and Whirlpool, which manufactures many home appliances such as dishwashers. Automobile manufacturing companies, such as Nissan, have also set up plants in the state, providing thousands of jobs for Mississippians.

Attractions and Landmarks

Numerous attractions across the state draw visitors to Mississippi. From north to the south, east to west, Mississippi offers sites to please everyone.

ELVIS'S BIRTHPLACE

Elvis Presley was born in Tupelo, in northeastern Mississippi. Today, visitors can see his childhood home at the Elvis Presley Center and Museum. Vernon Presley, Elvis's father, built the house with his brother and father in 1934. Elvis was born in January 1935, in the new home. The small, two-bedroom house has been restored to the way it looked when Elvis lived there in the 1930s and 1940s. The grounds surrounding the house include a statue of Elvis at age thirteen. The birthplace is a designated Mississippi landmark.

VICKSBURG NATIONAL MILITARY PARK

Vicksburg, in western Mississippi, was the site of one of the bloodiest battles of the **Civil War** (1861–1865). Today, the Vicksburg National Military Park and Cemetery contains more than 1,300 historic monuments and markers to Union and Confederate soldiers on the land that was once a battlefield. The park also features an

Vicksburg National Military Park was established by Congress in 1899.

Places to See in Mississippi

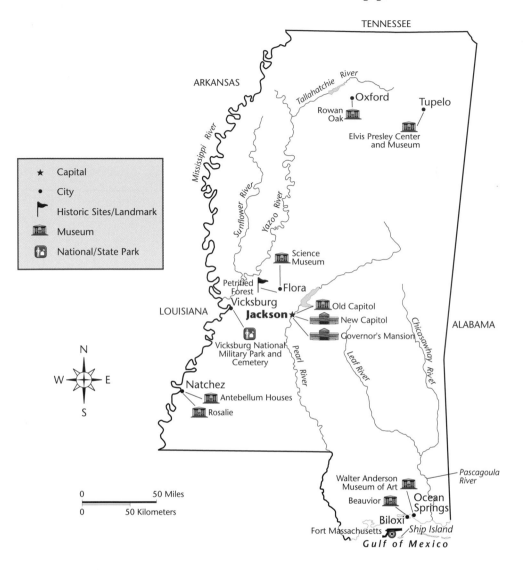

antebellum home, a sixteen-mile tour road, cannons, and the restored Union gunboat, the U.S.S. *Cairo.* Every state that lost soldiers at Vicksburg built a memorial. The Illinois State Memorial, built in 1906, is the largest memorial in the park. Its walls are lined with 60 bronze tablets that name each of the 36,325 soldiers from Illinois who took part in the Vicksburg campaign.

PETRIFIED FOREST

The Petrified Forest near Flora is home to petrified trees that are more than 36 million years old. The trees in the Petrified Forest were once normal trees that eventually **fossilized** and turned to rock. The fossilized trees were discovered in 1854, after settlers moved to the area and searched for good farm land. Visitors can also see the science museum while in Flora. The Petrified Forest was declared a Registered National Natural Landmark in 1966.

ANTEBELLUM HOMES IN NATCHEZ

Perched on the Mississippi River, Natchez is one of the oldest cities in the country. In the early 1800s up to the Civil War, the city was quite prosperous due to its cotton plantations. Many beautiful, large antebellum homes were built. More than 500 of these homes survived the Civil War and can still be seen and visited today. One such house is Rosalie. It is situated on a high **bluff** overlooking the Mississippi River. The French chose this site for the first settlement on the river in 1716 and it was named "Fort Rosalie" in honor of a French duchess. Rosalie was built by Peter Little from 1820 to 1823 and designed by his brother-in-law, James S. Griffin. Little had made his fortune in the timber industry and established the first sawmill in the Natchez Territory. During the Civil War, Rosalie was occupied by the Union troops. The dining room was the only room in the mansion damaged during the war. Union soldiers used it as their mess hall, cooking in the fireplace. The stains and cracks in the marble can still be seen today.

Future President Ulysses S. Grant led the Union forces that occupied Rosalie in 1862.

BEAUVOIR

Beauvoir in Biloxi was the retirement home of Jefferson Davis, the president of the **Confederacy.** The 52-acre es-

Beauvoir is now home to an extensive library on Southern history.

tate was built along the Gulf Coast between 1848 and 1851. Anne Ellis Dorsey was the original owner of the 52-acre estate built along the Gulf coast between 1848 and 1851. She named the home "Beauvoir," which means "beautiful view" in French. After the Civil War, Dorsey invited Davis and his wife, Varina, to stay in her home so that he could write his memoirs. They loved the house so much that they bought it in 1879. Davis lived in the mansion until his death in 1889. Beauvoir then became a home to veterans of the Civil War. Today, the home is a museum and memorial to Davis.

FORT MASSACHUSETTS

In order to defend its coastal ports, the U.S. War Department started building a fort in 1813 on Ship Island, just off the coast of Mississippi. The building of the fort took many years and was completed by the Confederates who used it during the Civil War. In 1861, Union troops took control of the fort. They used the island and fort to attack New Orleans and other southern coastal cities that were important to the Confederacy. During this time, they built the fort's hospital, barracks, mess hall, and many other buildings. Union troops turned part of the fort into a prison camp for captured Confederate soldiers. The Union troops named the fort for one of their ships, the *Massachusetts.* Before then, the fort had been referred to only as the "fort on Ship Island." The fort helped the Union defeat the Confederacy during the war. Today, visitors can take a boat from Biloxi to tour the preserved fort.

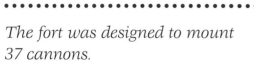

The fort was designed to mount 37 cannons.

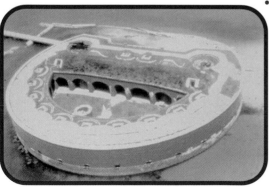

Map of Mississippi

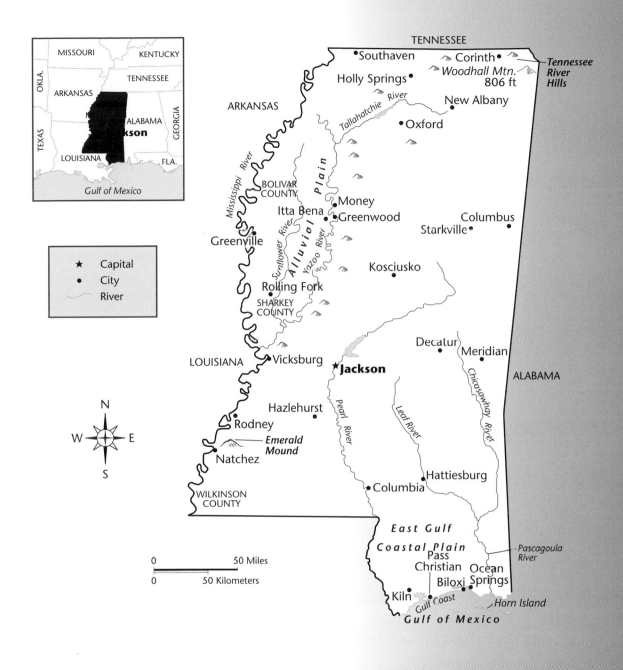

MISSOURI
KENTUCKY
TENNESSEE
OKLA.
ARKANSAS
ALABAMA
TEXAS
Jackson
GEORGIA
LOUISIANA
FLA.
Gulf of Mexico

★ Capital
• City
～ River

TENNESSEE

• Southaven
• Corinth
Woodhall Mtn.
806 ft
Tennessee River Hills

Holly Springs

ARKANSAS

Tallahatchie River

• New Albany
• Oxford

Mississippi River

BOLIVAR COUNTY

Alluvial Plain

• Money
Itta Bena
• Greenwood
• Columbus
Starkville •

Greenville

Sunflower River
Yazoo River

• Kosciusko

Rolling Fork

SHARKEY COUNTY

LOUISIANA

• Vicksburg

★ Jackson

ALABAMA

Decatur
• Meridian

Chicasawhay River

N
W — E
S

• Hazlehurst

Pearl River

Leaf River

Rodney •
Emerald Mound
Natchez •

WILKINSON COUNTY

East Gulf Coastal Plain

Pass Christian

Pascagoula River

Columbia •
• Hattiesburg

Ocean Springs
Biloxi
Kiln •
Gulf Coast
Horn Island

Gulf of Mexico

0   50 Miles
0   50 Kilometers

Glossary

alluvial a type of soil composed of clay, silt, sand, and gravel

ancient Greeks refers to the inhabitants of an important center of early civilization, Greece, from 1600–146 B.C.E.

antebellum existing before a war

archaeologists scientists who study the remains of ancient or prehistoric cultures

architecture the art of practice of designing buildings

artifacts an object remaining from a past period of time

bayous a wetland with trees, shrubs, or grass growing in or around it

bills drafts of laws or laws themselves

blues type of music developed by Southern African Americans with a slow tempo and often sad lyrics

bluffs high, steep banks of land

Civil War (1861–1865) the war in the United States between the northern states loyal to the Union and the southern states loyal to the Confederacy

climate the type of average weather of a geographical location, determined by temperatures and precipitation

Confederacy the eleven southern states that left the United States in 1861 and formed their own government

delta the land at the mouth of a river

descendant someone who comes from the same family of someone who lived years before

export a product that is sold to another country

fertile rich, abundant, productive

fossilized to become changed into a fossil, a living thing that has been trapped under the earth for thousands of years

French and Indian War (1754–1763) the war fought in North America between the British and the French which involved Native Americans as French allies; the British gained control of much of North America as a result

gospel music lively, up-tempo music heard in churches across the South

Great Depression period of American history in the 1930s when there were very few jobs and little money and food

humid condition when there is a lot of moisture in the air

memoirs memories and stories that people write about their lives

National Association for the Advancement of Colored People (NAACP) a civil-rights organization that was established to bring about social, political, and economic equality for African Americans through legal, legislative, and educational means

Nobel Prize for Literature annual award given out by an organization in Sweden to a writer of noted excellence

Oscar the highest honor given for excellence in film or movies in the U.S.

plantations large farms where crops are grown and where many people work the land

ports places where ships and boats dock and load and unload cargo

prairies fertile land that is flat or rolling and is covered with grasses but does not have many trees

precipitation water deposited from the atmosphere in the forms of rain, sleet, snow, hail, or mist

preside to direct, control

Pulitzer Prize an annual prize given to outstanding works in the fields of art, literature, music, and journalism

register a written record

republic a type of government in which people elect others to represent them and enforce the law

Revolutionary War (1775–1783) the war for American independence fought between the colonists and the British

secede to withdraw from an organization

segregation the act of keeping people of different races separate

siege a serious attack

surplus extra amounts

telecommunications the science or technology of communicating over long distances

temperate mild, moderate, not marked by extremes

valor bravery and strength of mind or spirit

veto to reject, usually a bill or law

World War II (1939–1945) war in which Great Britain, the U.S., France, China, and the Soviet Union fought and defeated Germany, Italy, and Japan

More Books to Read

George, Charles and Linda. *Mississippi.* New York: Children's Press, 1999.

Heinrichs, Ann. *Mississippi (This Land Is Your Land).* Minneapolis, Minn.: Compass Point Books, 2004.

King, David C. *The Battle of Vicksburg.* Woodbridge, Conn.: Blackbirch Press, 2001.

Ruth, Marsha Mudd. *The Mississippi River.* New York: Benchmark Books, 2001.

Shirley, David. *Mississippi (Celebrate the States).* New York: Benchmark Books, 1999.

Index

About the Author

Martin Wilson was born in Tuscaloosa, Alabama, and was educated at Vanderbilt University and the University of Florida. He writes articles, reviews, short stories, and children's books. He currently lives in New York. He has visited Mississippi many times, and his favorite place to stop is in Oxford.